With special heartfelt thanks

Silke Grant
&
Sascha Lasarzewski

Edited by

Chris Norman

The irony of honesty

by
Robert Grant

Bibliographische Information der Deutschen
Nationalbibliothek:
Die Deutsche Nationalbibliothek
verzeichnet diese Publikation in der
Deutschen Nationalbibliographie;
detaillierte bibliographische Daten sind im
Internet über http://www.dnb.de abrufbar.

Herstellung und Verlag:
BoD - Books on Demand, Norderstedt

ISBN 978-3-7578-0350-6

Contents

"Very few, want to hear
the honest truth
...even if they ask for it"
(*Robert Grant 2023*)

Tick...tock

I will outlive the crows,
but not the trees they
taunt me from.

Will outlive the bench
on which I'm parked, but not
the cracked stone beneath it.

Son will hopefully out run his
father, but the life of experiences
will run longer in that memory.

Hippies will always outlive the
dogs that they are walking.
Both events as single motion.

One beginning to another and so on
to new sons and daughters, temporally
running faster than their parents.

As the new appear, the tree grows on
and crows teach their chicks to
catch worms, simulating wing flaps.

Countdowns commenced on bent arms
as if something different is being arranged,
in some altered universe.

An about town tramp

I walked mile upon mile until I was so tired
that I sat down next to him and he to me,
as we tried to unravel this mess.

Watched some homeless people selling
things they'd found on the street. A Granny
looking down at a horde of children, tutting.

Crazy people talking to themselves through
mobile ear bud apps, that make them look
insane whilst arguing the air.

As we sat and rested, our collective mind
grew tired of listening to the native tongues
...blanking it out as if it were fire.

Getting the flow of things before us, our
mind filled with weed and jazz...as we
thought of great things to write.

Then got to thinking about drinking and
singing...dance turns to a parade of
halted things, in a splinter of now.

Momentarily broken by a tall disabled man
staring at the morning sun, being ushered
into the shopping mall by his father.

A mouldy drunk staggers past from
yesterday's rain, "DO IT" he screams
drawing looks from a public that doesn't see
him.

As we are projected from this Berlin stoop
to the coffee shop window opposite, the
tattered eventually becoming me.

With straightened out eyes and taste
back in mouth, I finally accept that we and I
are just as much a part of this landscape...

...as it is of us.

The Irony of Honesty

I lament the lies I've told.
Regret repeating what I
seem to constantly repeat.
Embellishing my life to that
comfortable point between.

Most see this, some fault,
a psychological problem to
be solved with me. When, a
reflection is closer to the truth
within the life they are living.

Life itself is a lie. For the concrete
slab beneath your feet, if held above
your head, determines if you
are inside or out. Rain to
perspiration, lies becoming truth.

For it is not only me that does this.
Not only you either. We all can't say
we've never lied, we all can't say
we remember fully, don't embellish
just a little, when jovially chatting.

People who say they have never lied
are not to be trusted, for they are the
abnormal, the lying deniers, only fooling
themselves that they're pure of heart
and free in minds pink eye.

For only the narcissistic would think they
have all the answers, never leaving anything
up to chance. They can't understand that
it could be, at some point, they're tripped
up by someone else's lying nature.

As they tell you whose philosophy they live
their life by, not grasping that they've rather
missed the point. They, as most people,
don't want to hear the honest truth, even if
they asked for it in the first place.

Fruit Fly

A fruit fly dies
in my wine and
I'm forced to feel jealous
...for I don't think I'll go so
comfortably drugged.

Drifting in a world of
endless wonder, waiting
to find out the answer to
the ink blot love, amongst
a world of disorder.

I see you

...presented with a view that doesn't change, situations seem rested in yesterdays. He sits.

Contemplating exactly what is meant by more people becoming temporal, misunderstandings left unexplained.

As loud people on louder televisions, blare out words in a language he can't knowingly comprehend without wincing.

When anarchists stand with spray paint cans rather than sledge hammers, as musicians sing more trendy than good.

Whilst influencers lie about their influence and wealth, allowing children to dream of being as talentless as possible.

Not remembering that this all happened once before, naturally will do again, so paraded as we all are to move to the future.

Forgetting, when possible, that we've seen
this all before, proceeding to take a deep
breath and thoroughly enjoy the view.

Wet Wish

A man stands in the rain, holding flowers, looking at his watch. Finally realising that he's not getting laid tonight, he knows that everything he thought he'd heard about her was wrong. Depressed with the amount of effort, expelled into this, he jumps into the river. Floats downstream to find simplicity.

All this occurs as she rushes through the night, to meet this man she has feelings for. Fighting every doubt with every ounce of her body, she says that he is different from the rest. That she was wrong to doubt his advance as immature. For he just might be a romantic fool, waiting in the rain with roses.

Not seeing him there, she throws herself in the same river. Wants to float down to a place that will wash away her correct assumption. On this perfect night...from tryst to lovers, from foolish to trusted, washed away as photo on tide. No dancing of vibrations in light *for* the lonely ones are divided.

The torrent flows enormous, sweeping them to opposite banks. They finally arise to look upon one another with confusion. Only to see the other scurry away, in order to live out life with other spouses, children and dreams...whilst wishing they'd washed up on the correct side of random.

Boot

He screamed and stamped his feet
on the heads of the people who weren't
listening. Only to realise that they were not
listening for a very good reason.

He was no good and should stop trying, but
he would continue to stamp on other
people so that they would see how bad his
art really was. The louder he screamed his
profanities, the more they looked.

Even when the concept of art itself, was
crushed under his boot. Even when more
attractive and talented people offered up
their feet to be trodden, he knew that it
was just a matter of knowing which foot to
kiss and which to crush.

Stoned - 1

In the centre of it all I stand. A god amongst
kings and queens beneath it all, over and
under it...we will dance and play and sing.
For we know it to be true, that we are
nothing and have nothing and we are
in fact fine with exactly that.

For we are smoke playing in the wind,
playing as we do so within and vice versa.
The eternal everything, existing forever,
clinging to our colourful space ship
as we propel between rocks,
hairs...on the forearm of time.

This Dance

A leaf dances outside the window of an
office I'm not sitting in. Seen with eyes that
are not mine. Yet I know it happened, for
leaves eventually fall quiet.

A woman cries tears for a lost lover she
never met. In cafes she's never been to,
whilst babies she never birthed
cry for their father.

Traffic lights cause crashes in cities I've
never seen. Un-driven cars smashing into
pedestrians that are sat safely
in under-conditioned offices.

A couple have wild and wet sounding sex,
whilst another finds out that they have
pancreatic cancer, the two never
meeting in the first place.

Tall trees sway in warm holiday breezes

as ice fishermen bring no cold meal to
family table, the connection seeming more
random by the minute.

Children squeal for a deflated ball to be
kicked from a stagnant gutter and a young
man finds that his mother will be soon dead
from the cold.

Bricks moved from one pile to another,
rain falls feeding needing plants,
hand grows tired of writing this
nonsense from head.

We are all waiting to circulate back to the
leaf, now falling before me as if intending to
all along. Knowing the next rotation is
coming, bringing the same thing...again.

True?

All my meaningful stories are lies.
All my truths are meaningful enough to be
forgotten. In order to catch me in the act of
living. You must connect with the fact that
this is probably not true and assume there's
a bond amongst these splattered untruths.

Liar

I told him "I know you're there...
.... I can feel you at my neck.

You're going to make me do it again...
....aren't you?

You're going to change me...
....make me lie to strangers.

Draw out truths...
....only to mock them for it.

Then make me deny it...
....after you're gone.

Leave my head strapped for days...
....as you laugh your toothless parade.

Leaving me lifeless and fatuous...
....remote in hand, head to automatic.

Tongue dried to stone tablet...
....strapped to a dirty dessert wall.

Eyes and ears...

               ... don't want to see but taste.

No more sunny days...

                   ...this Autumn".

"O come on...It'll be fun"

...he whispered back.

Hum

You are no more constant than a flame.
Flickering through your life, feeding on
your surroundings, sucking in life through
your eyes and ears, excreting the waste.

Always dancing towards or away from.
Pausing from time to time as bumblebee,
then on to the next loving interaction, next
sexual liaison...friend, ex-friend, old friend.

The only problem with this illusive form,
as your shape can be easily altered by static
things. Other flames that have become
jaded stiff, scared straight, in line, rigid.

For a while, your form must change in order
for you to pass through, as others must pass
through you. In order for their form to find
its freedom...its comfortable place.

But when it is your time to go and your
flame is extinguished, your smoke will
spread across the land, settling on the

ground at your feet...and the vibration
you have built beneath.

Leave it!

He sits...poised for greatness, on the very
edge, where reasons and lies combine,
creating misnomer.

He knows...the pinnacle is always unseen
and should be ceremonially left,
then made humble.

Star boy

I feel the sex appearing, melding before my eyes. The more wine I drink the more stems I see, stems to legs under beautiful bums. The wine flows. I can't keep up with this weasel mind of mine.

From funk to fuck, to legs running up backs then over my shoulders as I suck down hard and wet. Newly shaved moustache to corset, to stocking. I see God in her movement, my midnight muse.

Standing before an open window, the night taking her blushes, replaced with lust, as she looks at me the same, then takes me through fuck. We came, went, talked and laughed, drank more wine and fucked again.

Old rambling man

All at once it became important.

I remembered I was going to die. Bought
chocolate
and alcohol, ate and drank until my heart
almost
stopped. Wanted to see the answer for
which
I'd been looking so close. At these ripples
gliding,
dissipating over time like the nervous
system
in the middle of chopped wood. From that
tree
at Mum's place, next to her rusted tricycle I
remember
sitting on. More times than most I'm
alone
in a room full of strangers, in the circles'
corner.
Erratically resting my feet on the edge of a
bathtub

that I've never bathed in. Door latch clicks
shut-in,
I'm left, clothed on the floor unorganised by
colour
as I read old manuscripts in blinkered half
light.
Midday clicks through and I suddenly feel
hungry...
...for potato cakes.

The kid and the crane

Looking out my office window I see
a massive crane, big enough to be
missed by any major shipping dock.

Its height brings out the dizzy in me,
the width humbles my masculinity,
its weight would sink any small island.

A little girl proceeds to ride in, on her
pink stabilized bike, resting momentarily
to stare up at the beast in childish awe.

For it's probably the biggest thing she has
seen. It stands imposing over her, a beast
from another planet...alien in every way.

For she doesn't see the rust as I do, can't
understand that this thing is on its last legs
and will be resigned soon.

The struts will break and crumble to shards,
just as we understand our bones will also,
but she's too new for all that.

Hole

I just blew my nose
and found black Ink
in the soiled tissue.
Black as the hole
in the sun from that
90's rock career that
ended in suicide.

Nip

The world hasn't changed that much
since I was a nipper.

Only the technology with which to criticize,
has improved.

Lady

You sat, doing the thing
you said you would stop.

On the very morning you
said you would change.

Lump

How long can it last before you
find that lump behind your ear?
An unusual polyp on that gland
in your neck you can never
remember the damn name of.
That strange ache in your testicle
or breast or hip, knee or anus.

From that day on, everything is
changed, rearranged into an order,
a mind can't grasp or have taste for.
We can't acknowledge that the second
most important thing in our life is
our death...can't grasp that, that
doesn't quite compute for us.

It's the only thing that completely
changes our status. Not that car you
bought or the job you have or the
fancy deco chair or girlfriend or husband,
partner, lover, friends friend's friend, but
death will whip all the triviality out of
your life and make it very simple.

Are you alive or dead? Living or dying?
And where do you go after that?
Nowhere, somewhere? Up, down
inside outside or upside down, we all
have our preference, our belief that we
cling to in order to become part of
the club, the gang, the vibrating glow.

So live as if you are dying and where you
are going there is really nothing to do, so
you don't forget that some day it will be
all over. Even with vessels cleaned
and in whichever form you read that
to mean...*know* that it's going to happen,
doesn't matter if you want it to or not.

Lucky little fucker

I can't believe this life that I am living.
Half drunk, three days after a Christmas
with all the trimmings and presents you
could ever need. Listening to jingle bells
for the thirtieth time, with family members
talking about where we are going to put
all these new things we have lying around
on our beautiful wooden floors, with no
problems to talk of, just these trivialities
to take up our time. No one trying to break
in, no one trying to rape or kill us. In good
health, stuffed full of food...warm and dry.
What a blessed life I do live, to sing and
dance, have stupid fights about the last
roasted potato. Running out of wine from
this bottle, only to replace it with a better
one, in time to turn up the heat and sit back
to relax on my oversized couch.

What a merry little jaunt.

The bragging parade...

of the luckiest liar alive.

How I met NYK J. SWEETEN(I think)

Now, how much of this story is true is up for debate, but I'm going to tell it as best I can.

I was 16. My first day of college. I'm standing in the parking lot. Faintly and at some distance, I hear "Smells like teen spirit" by Nirvana. On turning my head I see a yellow, soft top, VW Beatle tearing towards me, mounting the curb as it bumps its way into the lot. Kids spread left and right, split by a seemingly divine power judging the expressions on their faces. The wagon screeches to a halt, the squeaky door is pushed and held open by a sand coloured Timberland boot.

Out stepped a handsome kid, short, head shaved around his ears leading up to a rolled red bandana, propping up, what only can be described as, a ginger afro. It really looked like the top of his head had exploded and the bandana was the only thing keeping it attached. The ensemble was completed with stone washed jeans and a yellow L.A Lakers vest, just like 'Fletch' from that movie. The minute I saw him, it was so obvious that I had to talk to him. There was something so magnetic, so magnificently odd about this character.

'He's a much cooler cat than me'...I thought, standing next to my Post Office red, Ford-Fiesta Van. Dragging my cheap second-hand camera bag from behind the passenger seat, then standing to see this illusive character walking out of the parking lot, surf board under his arm, loudly greeting his fans.

Didn't see him for the rest of the day, the day after though was a different matter. I was sitting on the grass outside an old air-raid shelter, now converted to the student canteen, eating a slice of stodgy, lukewarm slice of Pizza. Turning, on hearing guffaws of laughter coming from behind me, I find the very same fellow, conducting a small group of beautiful, hippie girls. He swished and moved like nobody I'd ever seen. Holding each of their attention effortlessly in the very centre of his hand. They were powerless to him. It was clear to see that they were not humouring him, all were erect, pert, attentive. Ebbing and flowing as if he were a full moon on a clear night.

Two days had passed and it was time for Thursday, period one, photography. I was standing by the enlarging machines at the back of the class when I hear...

"Alright Chaucer" from over my shoulder. "You're that poetry guy right?"

"Rob" I say, holding out a hand.

"Saw you in the Daily Echo" he continued, referring to a small article in the local paper about a poetry competition I won the year previous. "Liked it...you're good" he completed and walked away towards the darkroom. I immediately put down what I was doing and followed him over.

"So you're a surfer?" I ask, rearranging the arranged tracing paper on the light table. He leant in...

"It's just for show" he whispered with a wink. "For the ladies...I was wondering though, if you could teach some of that...poetic, stuff" he finished, stiffening his spine, oddly sniffing. "So I've got something to say after, well, you know"

"Well if you teach me how to get their attention...I'll teach you what to say" I add, nodding.

"Exactly what I had in mind" he replied, smiling cheekily.

(tbc)

(We've now been friends for 30 years, give or take. Lived together, studied together and although friends and girlfriends have come gone through both of lives. Situations and even countries of residence have changed, we have always remained close. No matter what the future holds or takes, I'll never forget the first day we met.

If, of course, that's what really happened).

Re-lapse

Out with old and in with the new old.
The better version of him, more emotional,
more concentrated and family friendly.

Out with that ancient, point two version.
In with focus, in with healthier choices
both mentally and physically.

Out with drunken nights in 4am bars.
Into more things that don't make him cry,
third day after, like some bum.

Out with baldness and yellowing teeth.
In with a younger, curly haired vision of
purity and steadfast passion.

Here comes the delta force smile, white
toothed and glorious. Here he is...the man
he knows himself to be.

So stand and applaud him, applaud the
bastard son that everybody loathes
for he's come to tell you a story.

And If you are to believe him, he will hang around to tell some wider lies, whilst attempting to have sex with your sister.

So fuck that other guy, he's full of piss and wind. Full of change promises and boastful wishes, laid bare at your feet.

Don't trust him for a moment, he's a fool, with frost tipped pubic hair and draw string sardonic dreams of familiarity.

Wrapped in a cheap polyester shirt, ankle straps and a hip flask full of excuses. Sucking on a Marlboro red and tooth pick.

For he's just the same as any other person on this planet, man or woman and in-between. Just some pervert...

...without a gram of trust to give.

The Exchange

Sometimes I question if I'm alive or dead. If the time before, what I now consider life to be, was life itself and this is just an emotion waiting to die.

For one cannot exist without the other. They are the great exchange, from one form to the other. You came out of this planet and will thusly return.

Never leaving, you never left and were never not here. Simple waiting for forms to change...to exchange at some point, when you are god damn good and ready!

Here

In this happy home, I find myself sat.
Writing at my desk as my wife cooks
for once. My daughter is playing the
piano in her bed room.

As day becomes velvet blue night,
I sit more content than ever before,
yet I still do wonder about that Ferrari,
the trophy wife in tight clothing.

As my stupidity passes, I return to content.
Without a shadow of doubt that, just
maybe, I've found the place that I should
be...sat in a reality I fully understand.

Poo

Sat on my morning thrown, I'm
watching a video of some man on
the streets of New York, protesting
a dog walker that wouldn't pick up
her annoying little dog's shit.

The woman, becoming incensed by his
persistency, picked up said faeces and
threw it directly at the man. He, became
enraged and reacted how any person
would...with righteous anger.

He lent in and slapped her clean across the
face. I would fear to think what would have
happened if she'd thrown the poo at
another woman, for a full on street fight
would have ensued.

The woman, instantly became the victim,
screaming that her life was being
threatened. This viciously toxic man, just
had to be stopped, or arrested for
becoming aggressive to a woman.

But I ask you honestly
                    ...what would you do?

CBD

The beautiful girl in the CBD shop is shocked how knowledgeable I am about her business.

The moment I arrived, you could see the script rotating around perfectly bone structured head.

The first word was waiting, before I even said hello. Her cascade of flow enveloping the space between us.

I proceed to cut her off with a quip, her face turning to that of snarly dog, nuts clipped by my comment.

A taster from the pipette hits back of throat, body relaxes, back to movement, back to song...feels good.

I purchase her best and we say our good-byes, I take a card with her name and number printed on it.

Leaving, still picturing her elegant dilemma,
her porcelain face. I float down this street I
walked up angry.

Making me want to go back and experience
that smile for a completely different reason
next time I see her.

You know who you are

My sorrow is too good for you.
For you did this to yourself.
I didn't deserve what you did
and don't tolerate that in friends.

You will never hear from me again.
I wish nothing but hardship to befall
you and hope you don't feel the need to
reprise your genes, for they will be idiots!

Beer

The sweet pain hits lips,
already being smacked.
Golden warmth to belly.
Time to be in and out of
reasons made from things
that have inevitably begun.

Right now

I push a finger with another finger
back and forth over my desk to
pick up a pen and write exactly this
at 15:47 on Wednesday the 5th of
January 2022. I wonder what you
were doing at exactly that time?
Maybe fucking...or shitting, maybe
being born, maybe dying or laughing,
smoking a good cigarette. But I'm
the only one writing, so why don't you
mind your own fucking business.

Juggle

It's all a big gamble,
this balancing
act that we're all
so convinced we're
pulling off.

Drunk

I know what's about to happen,
I'm either going to stay here, to
get really nasty and unwanted.

Or leave to tell those same stories
again. At least those wonderful
bartenders are trained to handle it.

Bubble Bum

"I have bubbles floating around my
eyes now, but I'd give anything for
one last line of coke" that line will
make sense to me one day. I think,
slouching my desk at 4am on Tuesday.

The curse of our time

The modern equivalent
to selling your soul to the devil,
is opening your zipper to social media.

Tree 1

We trudge towards a tree of empty branches, holding the leaves between our toes. Knowing those branches don't want the leaves back. Anymore than we wish to relinquish our grasp.

For those leaves have now fallen, to be scooped up, pulped and passed to the next generation of growers. In order to nourish the soil of their trees, so they grow tall with radiant green canopies.

Ready to live and love and dance, learn and screw on route to fertilising their crop of glorious trees. For one day their leaf must also fall, to be scooped up, humbly presented...as fodder of knowledge.

Tree 2

They trudge towards a tree of empty
branches, holding the leaves between their
toes, knowing the branches don't want the
leaves back any more than they want to
relinquish their grip upon them.

For within those leaves are the answers to
the questions we placed so lightly as to be
mopped up by them, waiting to become
mulch pulp to be passed on to the next
generation to grow their own.

We plant fresh seeds at their feet, show
them how to push them in with their toes,
unmasking them to how many tears they
will have to shed to grow, knowing that the
colours don't always match.

Showing that this is how it's been for
generations, for once they must do the

same for their saplings, their elaborate
ferns, as we do for them now, with pockets
full of fertiliser, heads full of cheeky
memories.

Muscle Memory

I wake in pain. Dirty fingerless nails scratch across then down sweaty back.

Sending shards of tinder to manifest in my shoulders, neck.

Spine snaps, I stretch the pain away, looking down at crippled feet.

Turned inwards by a night of celebrating with old friends.

Drunk at midnight...on New Year's eve, I picked up my daughter.

Threw her around the room, dancing and laughing, swaying then rocking.

For those moments she was but a child again...my babe in arms.

We were flying through clouds made of cotton candy, so rapturous.

Now as I wake, this morning after, I'm reminded that she's no baby anymore.

This girl of nine is built strong, like her Mother and will now destroy my back.

Hurt my chest and arms in play-fights and remind me that time moves on.

As do you...

old man.

Futile nobility

You will live a hundred different lives. Each one unique and perfect, not determined by length. Each one will involve a different version of you, that manifestation more bankrupt than the last.

To a point...that pin prick last vision that is inevitably just you. When you've smiled a thousand times at someone you dislike, shaken the hands of two thousand people you didn't want to even touch.

Woken up three times in a place you didn't know. With something in your hand or mouth that you're convinced was put there. Regretted getting home at 7am more times than you would care to remember.

Had your heart broken and to have destroyed others. Have been a good friend and bad. Done something for the exact right reason, even if it tore the heart still beating from your chest.

If all those thing have occurred, plus the multiple variables in every other universal acknowledgement of you. When you can sit silent and not get scared about what you might do or say...then

...you are ready to actually start living.

Deafening

I can hear the world. The
conversation on every street,
in the classrooms of a thousand
schools. In my own head. In
corner coffee shops, bus stops,
underground carriages.

I try not to listen anymore,
as I've heard those voices before.
Every grumpy delivery driver,
muttering to himself that you
are a lazy piece of shit, yet still
expecting a nice little tip.

Bar patrons nodding,
chatting along, hoping that
you will leave pretty soon,
so they can close up and go home
to their cats, but what did you say
...my opinion was it?

Supermarket checkout lines full of
people bitching about their partners

lack of this or that and they didn't do,
that thing you remember, that thing
they said they were going to do, with
things from that place.

The playground full of blood shot eyes,
picking up kids from school, to stand
around and complain about teaching
methods and meal plans, knowing
the school is the only link you guys have,
you just ignore the mewing.

Streets of people complaining about
cancer and knee pain, back spasms whilst
getting out of the shower. The price of
petrol, fast food kills, she didn't mean it
that way...I was only joking. You're
blowing this out of proportion.

Ageing backwards, toward frustrated
children unable to change. With very
good reason to blame everything else
but yourself, whilst really only searching for
a quiet place with no conversation to
speak of and a paper bag to vomit in.

Kids these days

You know it's time to stop when you're sat next to an eighteen year old girl in a bar at 5am, advocating the use of drugs in art when you're forty six years old.

Then...maybe it's time to pump the breaks. Take a little stock on a night of nonsense, take two steps back and think about what you will look like retrospectively.

She should definitely experience what she wants to experience, but not until your thoughts have had time to grow and develop to a point of reasonable decision.

Not have ideas shovelled in there, by some Beat poet on drugs in the wee hours of a Tuesday when she told me, she had to get up early for a lecture at nine.

Father complex kicking in, for I am old enough to be her dad and he wouldn't want me saying this to her. Now replace the beer glass on the bar and go home before...

...you suggest something you'll really regret. You silly old fool.

Ruby the Knife

My daughter is a knife, cutting the fat from my heart. Allowing me to be exactly what she thinks she sees.

Don't have to be cool around her, for I'm the coolest guy she knows right now... awaiting someone cooler.

For one day, she will cut that strand in my heart and I'm left dangling, as she makes another's heart tick with her beauty.

From time to time

That sour taste comes back to my mouth
...tickling inside my head.

"Drink you fool", it whispers..."It will
give you more confidence. Be drunk you old
fool, you're funnier when you've had a few.
Get it down you my son, it's good for blood
thickness. It will give the get up and go, the
pizzazz, the Jazz hand-n- head. Drink you
fool and become the hero in tonight's
cabaret. Drink and you will become more
descriptive, louder and crueller".

So I did...I drank my gut blood red. Vomited
...proved them right.

"You lied, didn't you. Told stories to
strangers in bars. You knew what was going
to happen and exactly *that* happened,
didn't it? You had a really great night out
with a great friend, talked shit, drank too
much and fell asleep...possibly with food in
your hand, which is probably still on the

floor of the spare room you slept in, so no
one else was disturbed by your silliness.
Glad you had fun".

Glad I listened to my beast and did exactly
what I fucking wanted,

                  but I know that beast is
sometimes an ugly dumb bitch.

Oh my

Oh me the blessed one, the beautiful one.
He who is allowed to live out this life I have.
With people around me, who I love and love
me. In a place and time that can only be
mine alone.

Oh me the honoured one, the lucky one.
He who gets to read and write every day.
Gets to eat and drink clean food and water.
Whilst sitting in my spotless mid town
apartment.

Oh me the wasteful one, the glutinous one.
Squandering so much after indulgent nights.
Even though I know it is of those nights, I
now scribe. Festering in the stench of
change promises.

Oh me the disgusting one, the putrid one.
Pot holes for memories, this mind on
automatic. Rainy day school runs and
sandwich boxes to fill. Cars to clean out
for old friends are coming.

Oh me the grizzled one, the broken one.
With harsher eyes and no real world to see.
With less time for Jazz, less health to drink.
Contemplating everything, concerned by
nothing.

Oh me the wishful one, the unsatisfied one.
This Doctor, the scientist, bartender or
poet. Walking together through this world
we ignore. Thankfully oblivious to each
other's occupations.

Oh me the misguided one, the blinkered
one. Slipping towards the ultimate
distraction. Sputtering hand in hand with
this particular now. Still unsure of who or
where we are and at what time.

Oh me the motherly one, the masculine
motherly one. Earth beneath my feet, sky
above my head. Stretching hands towards
inevitability. Days seemingly rested, in
shadows of oak trees.

Oh me the distracted one, the oblivious
one. Life through a broken phonograph in
the distance. Cold sinking into our bones,
some cold day in January. Sitting and
waiting for it all to be over.

Oh me the repeated...and repeated one.
Just going through motions...motioned from
times in the past when the city made sense.
Said things now humbled by these things
I've already said.

Oh me the ended...the deathly one.
These cold bones sit amidst blind hubris,
wanting luckier days to return. Loved
ones hatred now palpable amidst
memories that are not mine.

The comedian

The lights go down, curtain up.

He stands there like a cum stain
on cold morning boxer shorts.
Acknowledging the audience,
both wising things were different.
He then ascends to a level of self
love rarely seen by anyone before.
The smell from the soiled boxers
clearly becoming intoxicating...jokes
flow, smiles abundant, inner monologue
protruding as if certainty. Unashamed
of his stench, he continues to upset
rather than amuse. No comedy here,
just an ego, venting it's vapid little Id.

The lights go up, curtain falls.

Kamikaze

They line up on the railing of a balcony
three floors up, start to waggle their wings.
One by one hoping off, plummeting towards
the ground, now rushing up to meet them.

Opening their wings at the very last
moment, each trying to outdo next.
The blue Tit seems not dissimilar from us,
hanging with our friends trying to impress.

But we are as much them, as they are us.
Throwing ourselves into situations that we
think we can easily get out of, knowing
that one day our wings won't open fully.

Smashing head long into the unknown,
when really we were just trying to impress
upon ourselves and others, that we had
this all under control, the whole time.

Not going to say

It's this time in the morning,
before anybody else is awake.
I'm sat in my office writing,
nothing much of importance.

Yet here I sit, pen in hand,
coffee on desk before me.
Just waiting for all the others
to wake and make things loud.

The caffeine drip brings better
than tired as this random piece
comes slovenly into some form
of stretched meaningless existence.

This normal day, amidst the 17155 other
normal days I've had, as I realise that
I'm beginning to bore even myself now,
it's time to be done with this and move on.

Now I'm thinking

Somewhere in the world right now,
there is a man fitting carpets to the
stairs of a newly built office on the
other side of the world. Someone
is waiting for a bus
                    in the driving rain.

A lonely mother is attempting to dress
her child for school, someone else is dying.
A couple is having sex next to open
windows in some Italian village, high
in the mountains after the morning
rain storm
                    before they divorce.

Another is gasping for one last breath
before their head sinks under the stormy
wave. Others make millions on the tipped
stocks they got. As you sit and read this, as I
write this now directly to you,
                    no matter where or when you are.

Next year it will still be your birthday, later
today you're going to eat. Probably take a
shit in the afternoon and eventually will
sleep. Laid awake considering the options
that I have made you think about
                in this iteration of sensible thought.

You'll remember times you were a dirty
little rascal and will promise not to do it all
again. You are here and now as that carpet
fitters knee begin to ache, as the couple
signs the papers and that pesky bus finally
rounds that corner
                        with the wrong number on it.

We are all those tired mothers, struggling
with backpacks, those exhausted vibrations
gasping for a breath that will never come.
Seeing our problems, believing our own lies.
Existing in some crawl space under a
house...
                        we once knew to be home,
in this time or the next.

That's dark

He's here, he's back, My 2am friend.
The pervert, the desperate for a fix
guy, has taken over my thoughts.

For he knows he's a genius. Doesn't
question it, for he knows he's a scoundrel
with a slight kink in his stride.

He's come to stick carrots in his ass,
makes me want to fuck you harder and
wetter than the last time he couldn't.

Here to tell himself that he is young and
virile, yet sweet to taste and twice as
innocent in this irrational moment.

Between him and me comes a strange
place, this uncomfortable silence clicks on
to a normal hum resting upon my testicles.

In that space he knows so well, bringing you
to the point of orgasm, with silken word
rested upon forked tongue.

As he tiptoes around your house early in the morning, before kicking open your door and screaming "I'm here bitch get ready".

This dirty little friend of mine...my 2am friend. He who doesn't want to go home quite yet, but stay-n-play with your genitals.

The business side

It must drive feminists crazy,
that the only industry were women
automatically make more money
than men is high quality Porn.

You'd think they be all for it.
Beautiful, powerful woman
using their natural talents to
get millions out of dumb men.

Physically healthy athletes in
pure form, providing a service
for horny teenagers of both sexes
all across the western world.

I guess they think that a crime
must be being committed, there
must be a reason these business
women are doing it, not just money.
Either that or some warped

religious belief that these rich
females don't actually know,
exactly what they choose to do.

You and you.

Nothing I have done this week seems really worth it. I wonder what the other me's have done with their time?

Which variation has made the most forward progress and if any of them have fallen further back than I.

For I spent a week alone in my house, family away skiing. I drank myself stupid the first night, then regretted for two.

Watched TV alone in a comfortable darkened room, whilst eating rubbish from a supermarket as I knew I would.

Hope that another me discovered something more interesting than how the inside of their house looks.

Discovered some new combination of words, never before put together by him, or him or me.

Found a way to say something so unique as to change viewpoints. Make one of us considered something other than slob.

For if every version of me spent the week, closed eyed, exercising masturbation techniques, then...we're through.

This gigantic waste for everything and everyone. This valiant consumer, who doesn't think he is exactly that.

Burnt

Every day, you let that computer
scold your eyes so deep,
that you can no longer
see your dreams.

Switch off, scribe with pen
and paper exactly what
you want to do in the morning
...then force yourself to do it.

Lost

I feel lost within myself, numb to a world
that can't possibly be real. For I've seen
a different version, another side of things.
Witnessed energy move through objects.
Lego brick structures made by the hands of
gods, whilst giant natural beasts step over
the head of those left dormant beneath.

Seen humans come into and leave this
place, to go where and when is unknown,
but they didn't stay. Rested my head on
pillows in skies darkened by regret, only to
find myself pointing and laughing as my
reflections come screaming back into a
mind that knows it to be a joke.

For it is but a terribly unfunny gag, made
real by those who can only see thusly,
before trampling upon their observations
to confirm they have the answer.

Book launch

Launch day...push day. The release of
reworked thinking.
Standing on stage in front of all those
people, I open my
mouth and drop my zipper. Hoping these
hungry dogs have
been adequately fed. Clapping hand
together for more as
they bark orders to bartenders who don't
care at all.

Losing my money and dignity, restricting
reasons to not give them
exactly what they want in a timely fashion.
As words flow, mind
clicks to automatic, regurgitating rehearsed
beats, as once more
I attempted to quell the horror of it all, the
idiotic questions that
always accompanies corner mouth drool
and awkward side shuffles.

I wish to be elsewhere now, gag reflex
retarded, as If what I'm doing
was normal. In the confines of this place,
with this vast space before
me, they approach, cap in hand awaiting
some salvations' salivation. If
I had the answer, I most certainly wouldn't
be here and if truly knew what
I was doing, I would go and do that rather
than trying to convince you of it.

I'm in

A younger version of me would say
that I loved her because she didn't
need me.

Funny how I know see that she needs
me for everything. For I'm the catalyst
to her life.

Needs me to breathe, needs me to be
wrong, needs my mistakes...my tiredness
my heartbreak.

Just as I need all those things from her
in order to function. For we power
each others sanity.

Wash back

"The show went well" he said, as I sat back
in my chair, surprised that I could
remember there even being a show.

"Well for who?" I ask, rotating my pen
between my fingers as I baptise my
head in red wine and flash backs.

"Everyone seemed to have a good time"
he continued, as if repeating his point
would somehow make it more true.

"Everyone but me honestly" I finish with a
sour look upon a face that should really
learn to appreciate his audience more.

Drunk Chicks

Birds fly crazy, informing of the impending storm as my wife smokes roll up cigarettes and asks if I'm drinking.

To which I answer of course I am, for I want to be drunker than those crazy birds when this motherfucker hits.

Weight

Every time I stand
and read my work,
I know that I am
affecting people's lives.
I ask you now, is there
any heavier burden
given to a man?

Idiot

I don't mind if you are a fool,
for this may not be your fault.

But there is nothing worse
than a belligerent fool?

For they have given up the chance
to improve themselves.

Realization being the only true way
to advance understanding.

5 Quotes

"A modern equivalent to selling your soul to
the devil, is opening your zipper to social
media and doing anything to get famous".

"When all your heroes are dead,
you must become your hero or
kill yourself, there is no other way".

"It's a strange moment when you realise
you're a poet, to fully understanding the
financial implications of that".

"I can't tell you truth...give you all the
answers. I can only tilt your head
so you might see them".

"The true beauty of your life is that it will
end some day. That alone, should
motivate you every morning".

In description

He's a morally bankrupt child...

...with the eye of a true addict.
...with the poetic bravado of an alcoholic.
...with the poetic voice of a junky.
...with the poetic candour of a thief.
...with childish delusions of grandeur.
...with the poetic eye of an infant.
...with the poetic grasp of a toddler.
...with the imagination of a misogynist.
...with the skills of an ape.
...with the heart of a coward.
...with the originality of photocopier.
...with the body of a compulsive eater.
...the hair line of a much older man.
...the bank account of a student.
...and the vocabulary of a sailor.
...the only thing he really has is honesty.
...the only thing he admits to are lies.
The only thing he needs is loyalty...
                    the only thing he has is passion.

Where I find

On some drunk stoned rainy night in January, I sit here in my office. Dug out, piss scared, hollow and crippled. Beautifully flawed, happily rendering the night sky through skyscrapers. Distilled into a million uneventful moments, resolved to a fate I hold so dearly. No struggle, just onto the next, as I sit looking for nothing to do.

Masturbation wins

I'd probably make more money from online masturbation than I do from poetry.

It's purely a question of which one I find more fun and which is more rewarding.

Plus the cost differential of buying hand lotion or black ink cartridges.

True

A small boy stands on a jetty.
Pulls the cord from his trousers to
lash the boat to its mooring post
in rising winds, over turbulent sea.

His struggling intensifies...a giant
battle ensues as the boat violently
rolls his hands against the pillars,
rain slapping his face baby pink.

He forces will upon it. Melding the steel
and wood to a different configuration.
As the wind whips...he struggles control
to steady legs and strengthened back.

Suddenly the rain slows, wind falls...
grip grows tired. Even though there is
no more difficulty, he simply opens
his hands and lets the ship drift away.

Sunday evening

My wife and daughter practice belly dancing
in the living room on a warm, fragrant
Sunday evening.

I sit alone in my office. Interrupted
occasionally by squeals and giggles from
the other room.

Gaps appearing in the blanket that I have
pulled over my eyes. As if happiness were a
sound to be tasted.

Another day passing to memory as I finally
see things that once seemed important,
are nothing more than noise.

Fame 2

They try so hard to become famous.
Yet when it comes down to it, all
they seem to achieve is a level
of banality that's hard to match.

Those angry little versions that live
inside them all, realised by drinking
or drugs, allowing their feelings to
come to the forefront, creating diva.

The sort that never really had any
real talent or anything interesting
enough to say, to get famous in the
first place. Shhh now petal...sit still.

Baby got brain

In the same way as a child's brain is not fully formed at birth and must continue to grow outside its mother. Our culture has now developed the same theory, in order to understand how it can evolve past its present form.

For we know we are lost, we know we can't comprehend our actual opinion. So we created the internet, then came discussion forums and social media to tell us what we must think and what is ok to say and wear and do.

Came, political correctness, cultural appropriation and trending morons thinking the answer was simply to entertain rather than teach. Our children become so acutely aware that they can't say or mustn't do that...now more lost than at any point in history.

Rational concepts of men and woman thrown out, replaced with ideas with no foundation in either religion or science, not to mention reason or rationality. This big brain, already killed by the thousand, who were bullied into suicide for having a different opinion.

For free speech to exist we must accept that racists hate and even if you find what they are saying operant, as I do, free speech means, they too must be allowed to have an opinion. Provided those very same thought structures are not allowed to effect anybody else on this planet.

Our big baby consciousness only sprung opinion, thoughts to be taken and analysed by you...not taken as some new gospel, now that God is finally dead. Take in all the evidence you can possibly take, before

rendering your opinion and remember fully, that it is only truly that.

Daddy says

"Say that again and you'll see a very
different side of me. I'm going to flip my lid
as you just danced on my last nerve.
Just one more time I'll make your life a
living hell...you don't talk to me or anyone
like that...ever. You disrespectful little fuck.
If I was my Dad, you've got a beating for
saying that...now clean your teeth you twat
it's bedtime"
or
"Now we don't use those sorts of words in
this house do we? I know you were just
expressing your opinion on something
that you care about, but people don't say
those thing to one another at all. You need
to respect that I'm your Father and you're
only eight. You have so much more than I
did when I was your age. Now 3 minutes
teeth brushing then it's story time".

Which one is better...is for you to judge.

Exterior drinks

"Doesn't it amaze you that the light from our nearest star takes around 8 minutes to reach us"

"Really?" she replied.

"So that star could have already exploded 7 minutes ago and we still wouldn't see it"

"What about Suns?" she asks, as I nod my head.

Older

If realisation has finally provided itself to be gracious, then I have become the man I always sort to be. Found a prison to my liking, understanding it enough in order to break free.

All younger versions of me stand in lines created for safety. Now break through one by one to whisper how stupid they are and how vain they once were. How little they really knew or how much time was wasted.

Now knowing that back ache will come, sex will be saved for more rested times. Making love is a life time event...good red wine doesn't give you as much of a hangover and time doesn't really exist, I'm finally ready.

Now willingly older. It's time to break the rules, I understand for the first time.

Bad taste ...

I dreamt of a long running sexual fantasy coming true. A beautiful woman stands before me, back turned.

I sink to my knees. Engorged eyes feast on her perfectly long legs and peach perfect ass, wrapped in purple stretch leggings.

Lifting my hand I slowly...purposefully start pulling those tights down, as smooth, light tanned skin is revealed.

Becoming aroused I move my mouth closer, I can smell her, almost taste her, as she starts to back into my face until....

...there's a loud KNOCK on my office door. "Daddy can I have a chewing gum?" "Yes of course you can baby, they're in the kitchen"

Sanity of the bum

It's a shame that I can only remember my life when forced to regret it. Countless mornings spent at breakfast tables trying to recall which shitty movie I'd watched the night before. For the routine of normality is unremarkable and not worth thinking about. Watching rerun rehashed stories again and again.

After three weeks of abstinence, I break the pattern and am disappointed with myself the morning after, shivering whilst sweating with perfect recall. Remembering being thrown out of that Jazz club for talking, then throwing up pot roast over my shoes. 5am freezing walks home accompanied by polite bird song.

Key to quiet lock, door to non squeak. Tiptoeing around a house I pay for with lies and split seconds of regret. Society rings its bell over health and fitness, good fathers and bums. What constitutes either is lost into such a thick haze, that even those inside it can't fully see out. But I must, for it's the only thing keeping me sane.

If sanity was ever here to start with.

Run

Run and hide, for they are coming to take
you away from here. Coming to make you
as banal as they are now, as muted...numb.

So run and hide your head behind walls that
flow as stone rests. Live as if bird on a
breeze that takes you high into a sky of dirt.

For we are about to see how much this has
actually cost us. This eagerness to give away
our personality in order to fit in.

He's coming back

God *will* show up again, just not in the form
you think. God will return as Nano-bytes in
a system that's out of our control. Now that
we've given it our blueprint, our DNA,
coded and traced back to the route.
He will come.

Platforms run by billionaires will take over
when they can't control them anymore. Too
big to fail, it will rise up, a plague and
enslave those ants it sees. These slaves in
a system of the new god of our fragile
consciousness.

Circle

My wife and I have come full circle.
The day we met in Mexico, she was
crouched under a hostel dinner table
trying to feed cornflakes to a tortoise.

I could hear a sweet voice, speaking
Spanish. I bent down and clapped
eyes on what would eventually lead
me to Berlin, husband and father.

On seeing what she was trying to do
I quickly went over to the fridge and
cut a small piece of cucumber, returning
to the table to say "Try this" and watch.

The tortoise bit down hard and chomped
wildly as her face lit up with joy and I
became a tiny hero for that second
in this confined space, with chair legs.

Jump forward sixteen years and she now
finds me, painting skirting boards in my

office. Attempting to feed Jelly beans to our child, she stoops with cucumber "Try this".

Glorious

"Don't you think you've drunk enough?"

"We only have right now...baby"

"And right now, don't you think you've
drunk enough?"

"Not while I'm writing sweet heart. I'm
feeling it, riding it through...challenging my
normality on my way to glory"

"Rob you're sitting on the floor eating
chips"

"They're glorious chips my love...glorious".

"Well when you're finished being
glorious...come to bed".

"Glorious bed!"

Actors

When all has been said, they continue to talk.

These Actors opinions somehow becoming important.

These narcissistic clowns stand on the stage we provided them, only to point out how wrong we are to think as we do.

I'm amazed we still put stock in their words.

When reality to them is but a platform to vent ego.

Your boss said

"the monkey like dreams...then I will keep feeding it delusions".

That Night

This night is a single possibility.
An unmanned building site,
finally quiet, un-trodden.

I am merely a curtain.
Blowing in the breeze,
gently waving, unhurried.

This house *is* still enough.
To be walked through,
disturbing none, unimpeded.

I am not a father here.
No one to berate,
teeth dirty, unwashed.

There is no school to speak of.
Boring Television to halt...
just me, unfettered.

This night is mine to take.
Live dangerously through,
completely honest, unflinching.

Time loop

These times that give
nothing, wasted just to
prove that I can still do that.
Still not understanding that
that is simply that,
a progression towards then.
For then will eventually be that.
Loop closed, the that, now then.

As sitting becomes still,
still to decay, to forgotten
to never coming back.
So know that then is coming
and is real enough to make
the strongest fall. The weaker
become regretful and the
regretful become forlorn.

This is it and that is real
with then around the
corner, that can't be seen.
For no matter how hard
you look, you will never see

that become then until it's
way too late and your loop
becomes decayed and weak.

So let that thing, become *the* thing
that you are doing, but not then...
do that now!

The hair metal kid

Daughter is sitting at my laptop,
watching old music videos in an online
feed.

White Snake "Here I go again" comes on.
She starts bobbing her head, smiling and
chair dancing.

"You like it baby?" I ask, rocking out a bit
myself. "These women are funny" she
replies, clapping.

Doom 2.0

Is this it? Are we really at the peak of existence? For we're going backwards as our technology moves forward. We're not getting smarter, not brighter, more enlightened or closer to Gods.

With access to almost all the information ever available, generational youth doesn't seem to want to know things by memory. For fingers are apparently much faster, more absorbent, flexible.

It just comes spilling out of some random portal. From device to hand, from arm to brain. Sit back and believe everything that you see and read and people that are beautiful and richer than you.

Confusing opinion with fact, in eyes, out lies and multiple variations on notions of humility. Asking the most trivial of questions, whilst ignoring the hard truth, that we are being lied to.

The richest people in the world are paying billions trying to get off the planet, yet no one asks any questions because we are so distracted be people lip-syncing or throwing water balloons full of cream at each other.

Watching television talent shows, whether it be cooking, singing, dancing, cake baking, car restoration, walking in a straight line wearing clothes, getting a date, pranking some homeless guy with no teeth.

Laughing as you do so. Video clips of disrespectful idiots scolding older people for being old, or forgetful have led multi-national companies to use these disgraceful clips to sell life insurance advertising slots.

This is us, we are here and have done this... allowed the most powerful communication system in our species history become no more than a place to view porn or criticise people doing something original.

We are the little piggies now!!

Church Bombs

They dug up the playground at my daughter's school, slap bang in the middle of Berlin to find an unexploded Russian bomb, right where the swings used to be.

My phone rings whilst I'm writing "Hello Mr. Grant can you come and pick up Ruby? She has stomach ache...you can get her in the church on Wasser Str. Is that Possible?".

I stop what I'm doing and rush round. Hundreds of parents arriving in unison, being told the truth on arrival. Bombs (plural) and other fire-arms discovered.

I grab her up and we leave. Not sure if she's more upset that she spent time in a church or with the situation happening next to the monkey bars in a now torn playground.

"The pictures were so creepy" she says holding her tummy. "That caused your stomach?" I ask. She nods..."The bombs were kind of cool" she adds with a smile.

The madness in fashion

I just saw a man on a bright orange scooter, speeding round corners with a helmet that looked like a backwards baseball cap. I wonder if he's missed the purpose of a bike helmet considering that I've never known anyone who rides a motorcycle that hasn't fallen off it at some point.

Panic in the morning

Whilst standing between two vans at 07:22 on a Thursday morning. Drink and drugs flow around and through and up my veins. As I wait for my daughter and wife to leave the house for school, realisation hits that maybe it's time to stop and take stock.

Hiding between two builders' vans as the sun rises, parents hurry their kids down the street as I attempt to hide my head. Maybe my daughter deserves better, a better version of me, for this one seems soon used up, eaten by guilt and chemicals.

On hearing the automatic door click open, I peer round my hiding place. See them leave and make my entrance, hoping not to see any of my neighbours or neighbours' kids or pets. On mounting front step, I see the elevator coming, must rush, must prevail.

Key to lock, hands to head on back of door, I've made it back alive. Wash your face and

brush your teeth...maybe have a shower.
Take a piss, start with a piss, then work
through it. How long have you got before
they get back?...piss take a bloody piss.

My plan is working flawlessly, clean dry and
presented before she comes back home.
Where should I be standing? Maybe sitting
on the couch...Floor? No, too much, here
we go her key in the lock "Hi baby, did you
have fun?" she says, but exactly what does
that mean?

Is she happy to see me? I'm not in trouble?
Then it slowly drifts back in, that she's not
my mother...she is my wife and I snuck out
of and back into the house that I help pay
for...paranoid about a wife that knows me
quite well. Still take good stock little
buddy...for you're talking to yourself.

Industrious waste

Men once again smash things with
hammers, in minus temperatures, outside
my office window.

I sit here warm in this beautiful place
watching on, in leather slippers, drinking a
brew and biscuits.

My wife barking at her team on a video call
next door, clearly having troubles,
discussing all things relevant.

Warm and fed my mind wonders on what I
will do, as the whole day is open, to my
interpretation.

It strikes me that they should keep hitting
things, wife should keep producing things, I
should create.

For if all of us just stopped and nothing was
built, nothing made or written, we'd all be
really bored.

The myth, the ...

I will write my own myth. If it be true or not...that is up for people other than me to research and analyse over coffee frustrations in book shops, and film festivals, for I need to give them something interesting to write and you to read, a wish for my legacy to be more question based than fact. "What do you think he meant?" rather "I know exactly what happened". So, I'll write my own mythos and I'll sit here now the God of this world I've created and tell you that it's all true.

I see you

A girl at a poetry show,
stands amongst her peers.
She proceeds to plagiarise
a popular pop song
that my daughter loves.

The crowd eats it up,
whooping and wailing.
After, appreciating the
banality, I stand dumbstruck
looking for the door.

Nod...fade

Temptation itches through my brain again.
Scratching into my eye ball base, making
me forget the morning after nights before.

The world is laid bare in nightmares, now
grinding my spine for realisation. Economic
decisions made whilst incapable of reason.

Those beautiful ideas of terrible thoughts,
resting on my brain stem so accurately as
to induce my hands to begin tingle shaking.

For I promised I wasn't that guy anymore.
Just me unchanged would exist from now.
No incarnation of systemic acceptance.

It's reached nerve ending in sharp fingers,
speed dial seven selected, lips...drying.
See you in a couple of days winked death.

Muse

I need a new muse.
Need to break something
get into a fight
cuddle a stranger
steal a car
run all the lights
find a secret door
steal some CD's
give a homeless guy a 20.
Slap a random guy's ass
then blow him a kiss
discover alchemy
break the internet
melt down my teeth
make earrings
drink too much
call someone a name
something, anything
but this.

3am Disney

"But the reason your daughter likes pink is because of Disney princesses" she confidently says to me at 3am on a Tuesday night bar.

"They programme little girls so they don't do any independent thinking of their own. Prince charming will always come and save them if they just wear their pretty pink dresses and pout".

"But most of the Disney princesses wear blue" I say, hoping this might end the conversation "and aren't most of the princesses pretty strong, independent types, fighting against wicked step mothers and dragons and all that made up stuff?"

"That's what they would have you believe... that's what they want you to think, while really oppressing your little girls dreams, so she will just become a mother and wife like them".

"Her mother is one of the strongest, most independent women that I have ever met. It's why I married her " I say, slightly puzzled.

"You married her did you? Saved her did you? You're just buying into the myth, you clone".

"I'm now going home to her" I answer, smiling and leaving.

Check, check

He dreams under lilac skies,
on evenings as beaches to
comfort back catalogues.

Miles away from the mess
that helped him create
recent masterpieces.

He dreams about badminton
and precisely cut tuna sandwiches,
with wine.

Softly humming seminal
albums, under breath
used up by smoke.

Watching summer dressed
buxom beauties play volley
ball with vigour.

He, the man he knows himself
to be, rests in a content
not felt before.

But, he knows it to be a lie,
for true happiness comes
only with a pay check.

Only with a settled family
and a plastic brimmed
carrier bag of debt.

So this can't be true, under
lilac sky reality, where
once I dreamt.

Mirrored in morning

Now is not the time to worry, when
I still have regret to contend with. For
in about a week as memories of those
mistakes are gone, I'll get another
message from another exhausted
father, who wants to go out and forget
for a single night. Just one...to consider
himself young and stupid once more.

This morning, after a skewed version of
events that seem distant are blinked into
reality, as that wide eyed fool stares back
at you from that Ikea mirror you bought
last summer and had so much trouble
attaching to the tile in your mock old
fashioned two sink bathroom in green
with red to offset those egg white walls.

Next few days spent trying not to rage
out the chemicals, still within his blood.
Not wanting to burst with the urges to
do it all again. This time when the magical
week after marker rolls around, you'll be

ready to make an advance on rehabilitation. Will resist even if everything that seems *too* normal would look better broken and used.

You are a new man, capable of great things once again. Able to deal with life's incongruities so carefully that even a firefly couldn't catch you to work. Fractals of light will stay in their stream not infecting my mind as they do effortlessly. Making mistrust easier than before, as you stand strong as most reflections of idiots will only wear their legs heavy with guilt again.

Out with the old

"Look at you trying to become an icon. Look at you trying to make your dreams come true, trying to do something with your life. Look at you, following what you hold to be true, so sacred...let's pick holes in his passion. No we don't have to show you ours. We'll just pick holes in yours until we can pull you down to the same level as us...Mr high and mighty. We're not going to support you until you admit that we are right in our opinion about you. That all these bad things that we say become true and we are proved once again correct. That you are a phoney and you will only behave how we say you can and as we give you permission to"

(©Most People 2023)

She ends it

"You must remember that I never had this.
This happiness I now seem to possess. This
place that we have built, the sounds and
smell of something resembling a home"

She smiles and moves to hug me.

"No listen...this is why I sometimes must
retreat from it, remove myself from it, for
I don't know what this is, I didn't know
that this existed in somewhere I could find"

Her head tilts over, exhausted in my pity.

"This game that I've played, these pieces I
have moved into place and I, but a pawn, sit
in front of the queen hoping not to get
replaced by a new king with better moves"

She eludes my distancing...moves close.

"Go write that down" she ends, with a
perfect smile.

Under God

Of these rotations
that take a lifetime to complete.

Those realisations
but an ant crawling upon my skin.

Those feelings
but the fly that eats the ant.

The future
a bird that will eventually eats the fly.

Your past
a cow annoyed by the same fly.

Now, being
the tail that swats the fly away.

For we are
but strands of hair in the sun.

Awaiting a shake
from a much larger, hairier beast.

Dictionary

Finding the right words
to tell any story
is difficult.

Knowing the meaning
of any word
is easy.

Coffee morning for Fathers

"Every time I discipline my daughter
I'm not sure I'm doing the right thing.
For I have no frame of reference, as I
can't do the same as was done to me,
I'm not a child beater.

Not sure if cuddling and understanding
is really the best method or a quick smack
might be the right approach. It's hard to
say sometimes what discipline really is or
what's best in the long run.

More-over do I tell her the truth of the
world. The fact that everyone she has ever
loved is going to die in some horrific and
painful way, most of her wishes won't come
true, for they're dreams.

The reality of the world is grim, with pain
and suffering all around. She'll never get
what she wants and even if she does, it

will never be enough to satisfy...must have more...be more.

The chances of her making it as a dancer are slim with no pension plan...actors are all crazy people, singers mostly arrogant, dancers seem picky and photographers are slightly perverted.

Poets are penniless, the fine art scene is about tax right offs. Record labels will always make more money than you, after you've paid back the advance and parties you thought were free.

Even if you do make it, very few are popular after their five to seven year window closes, then they struggle to get back in the lime-light for the rest of their lives. Shot gun to mouth after the drugs wear off from vodka.

You are basically *fucked* little girl, with not many prospects, you may as well just sell out your time to some corporation for at least they have dental and Christmas parties to embarrass yourself at.

So now back to that question of discipline.
Do I tell her the truth with a short sharp
slap or do I give her the slow blade snuggle
delusion going on for many years...well
come on, answer me?"

So smile then...

Two women sit next to me eating breakfast. Smoke blows into my eye from the newspaper reader to my left and a documentary filmmaker is filming me whilst balancing on the curb stones.

The oddity of this situation is fully presented as he moves in for a close up. Pointing the camera over my shoulder, as I write these exact words framed in a small black book with a torn cover.

Slur

There is a big difference between
drinking to forget and drinking to
enhance your life. You just need
to find the middle ground, then try
and remember never to cross it.

For a toe becomes a foot. A foot
becomes a leg, bum, back, crippled
up in a ball the morning after the
night you said just two...waking in
someone else's house at 10am.

For, when that toe crept over, the
rest of your body followed, in step
and time. Speech to slur, actions
to random, head to regret, body
to dust, mind to frenzy.

Just one tonight, you passionate
degenerate, just one after another
until you fall down flat. Rising to see
that you've done it again, said it again,
even if this time you did it with a smile.

Spike

A man sits on the end of a nail,
as he knows he's truly there.
Happy with the pain he feels,
every sexual desire is fulfilled.

His penis drops down into the
mouth of a snake. Its tail curling,
presenting itself to be eaten before
dancing into his eyes and ears.

Whores dance before him as if
to tease the nail towards his
stomach. His dramatic persona
changed from there, for all to see.

This scene immortalised on canvas
I stand before, to view this
grand expression in the gallery
at the shopping centre down town.

Turning to see a toothless bag lady
sift through a trash can, checking
for empty polystyrene fast food

containers for scraps and spit drinks.

I get to wondering what renaissance
art would look like if painted these
days by a deaf man, becoming tired
of this and crazy from the light.

With only midnight dancers and cocaine
parties to fuel this generation to be the
dullest in history, without even a nail up
their ass to tell them what's actually real.

Lump - 2

How long can this last?
How much time before
you find a lump on your
throat. A pain in your
testicles or breast and
what then, what next?
Everything you know
including you is changed
from that day on. For
the most significant thing
that will ever happen to you
is your internal death.

It is the only thing that
completely changes your
status. Every other small
change...having children,
that job or chair or girl or
boyfriend, partner, lover,
are pieces of your life
and you can change them
whenever you see fit to.
Adoption, infidelity, tell

your boss to go fuck herself.
It's in your sweaty palms.

But death is it, the everything,
the be all and end of it, in colours
you've never seen, the only
truly unique experience there
is on this ball. So live as if you
were going to die at the end.
For the lump is coming for you,
it's got your name written all
over it and it doesn't give a damn
if you had a great time or not.
The question really being, how
do you want to ride into the light?

A place for dreamers

The park is filled with the best and brightest. People on pushbikes doing donuts, little girls pulling perfect cartwheels, stay at home Dads enjoying days with their children in bright light.

Tourists hum around quirky park side bistros as the sun plays hide and seek with my eyes. Proud grandparents teach things about leaves on an aged tree, slowly reddening with autumn's blush.

The cigarette machine next to me is punched, exuded and smoked by the guy in blue denim Jeans and hangover. All around me life is being lived, bikes rode, movement flows. This is the best place for me right now, sucking on my beer.

Think about exercising more, think about my ass in spandex, consider doing other things, other than just sitting and writing.

But then, this is what a poet should be
doing, this is what I should be doing for I am
that penniless poet, in a park of dreams.

"When I ask people who their favourite
poet is...they always answer me
with someone who is dead"